Wandering Albatross

by Grace Hansen

Abdo Kids Jumbo is an Imprint of Abdo Kids
abdobooks.com

abdobooks.com

Published by Abdo Kids, a division of ABDO, P.O. Box 398166, Minneapolis, Minnesota 55439.
Copyright © 2022 by Abdo Consulting Group, Inc. International copyrights reserved in all countries.
No part of this book may be reproduced in any form without written permission from the publisher.
Abdo Kids Jumbo™ is a trademark and logo of Abdo Kids.

Printed in the United States of America, North Mankato, Minnesota.

102021

012022

THIS BOOK CONTAINS
RECYCLED MATERIALS

Photo Credits: Alamy, Getty Images, Shutterstock

Production Contributors: Teddy Borth, Jennie Forsberg, Grace Hansen
Design Contributors: Candice Keimig, Victoria Bates

Library of Congress Control Number: 2021940122
Publisher's Cataloging-in-Publication Data
Names: Hansen, Grace, author.
Title: Wandering albatross / by Grace Hansen
Description: Minneapolis, Minnesota : Abdo Kids, 2022 | Series: Antarctic animals | Includes online
    resources and index.
Identifiers: ISBN 9781098209421 (lib. bdg.) | ISBN 9781098260132 (ebook) | ISBN 9781098260484
    (Read-to-Me ebook)
Subjects: LCSH: Wandering albatross--Juvenile literature. | Sea birds--Juvenile literature. | Birds--Juvenile
    literature. | Birds--Behavior--Antarctica--Juvenile literature. | Zoology--Antarctica--Juvenile literature. |
    Antarctica--Juvenile literature.
Classification: DDC 591.709113--dc23

Table of Contents

Antarctica

Antarctica is the southernmost continent. Nearly all of Antarctica is covered by ice. It is one of the coldest, driest, and windiest places on Earth. But some amazing animals still live there!

Africa
South
America
Antarctica
South Pole
Australia

Wandering Albatrosses

The wandering albatross is an incredible seabird. Its **wingspan** can be more than 11 feet (3.35 m) in length. This is the longest of any bird. It can **soar** for hours without flapping its wings.

Wandering albatrosses are
known for their long hunting
trips. They can be gone for
up to 20 days. They cover
thousands of miles. This is
how they got their name.

Wandering albatrosses have white body feathers. Their wings are dark in color.

They have dark, round eyes.

Their **bills** are large, pink, and

end in a hook. The hook makes

it easy to grab food.

Wandering albatrosses mainly

eat fish and animals like squid.

They will make shallow dives

to grab their food.

These seabirds are rarely seen
on land. They do come together
on land to **mate**. Then they form
large groups to nest.

Baby Wandering Albatrosses

Wandering albatrosses often **mate** for life. Females lay a single egg. The parents take turns keeping the egg warm. Chicks hatch after about 11 weeks.

Parents again work together to care for the chick. One keeps the chick warm and the other hunts. Slowly, the parents spend more time away. After many months, the young bird will be ready to fly!

More Facts

- Scientists believe wandering albatrosses might be able to sleep while **soaring**.

- These birds have a surprisingly good sense of smell. Scientists think they can smell food from up to 12 miles (19.31 km) away.

- Wandering albatrosses can live for more than 50 years!

Glossary

bill – the parts of a bird's jaw that form the beak.

mate – to come together to have young.

soar – to fly or glide in a swift, easy way.

wingspan – the distance from the tip of one wing of a bird to the tip of the other.

Index

Visit **abdokids.com** to access crafts, games, videos, and more!